"Multiple Stories:
A Collection of Heartfelt Tales"

AF410058

BlueRose ONE
Stories Matter

First Published by

ISBN: 978-93-5741-396-1

BLUEROSE PUBLISHERS
www.bluerosepublishers.com
info@bluerosepublishers.com
+91 8882 898 898

samanwit2009@gmail.com

About Author:

Samanwit Kumar is a multi-talented individual with a passion for writing and acting. He currently works as a Project Manager at a Telecommunication company in Navi Mumbai, India. Samanwit holds a Master of Business Administration degree with a specialization in Information Technology.

Apart from his professional life, Samanwit is deeply involved in his hobbies. He has a great love for writing and acting, which he has pursued through various courses and certifications.

Samanwit completed an acting course at Actor Prepares in Santacruz, Mumbai, where he honed his skills in stage and screen acting.

He also completed a course in writing at Whistling Woods International in Goregaon, Mumbai, further expanding his knowledge and expertise in the field.

Samanwit's love for drama and theatre led him to participate in a drama course at the National School of Drama in New-Delhi. He also participated in drama productions at Manju Shree Natya Munch in Gorakhpur, Uttar Pradesh.

With his diverse experiences and talents, Samanwit has become an accomplished writer and actor. His passion for storytelling has led him to write engaging and thought-provoking stories.

Through his writing and acting, Samanwit aims to inspire and entertain people while exploring various themes and ideas.

Overall, Samanwit Kumar is a dedicated professional with a passion for writing and acting, whose diverse experiences and talents have shaped his unique perspective and style.

Dear Reader,

I am excited to introduce my book ("Multiple Story: A Collection of Heartfelt Tales"), which is a collection of short stories that I have written to share my own thoughts with you. Each story explores different themes, emotions, and experiences that we all can relate to. These stories are written in a simple, yet powerful language that will take you on a journey of self-discovery and introspection.

In **"MAA: A Mother's Unconditional Love,"** I delve into the immense love and sacrifices that mothers make for their children.

"WOMEN'S DAY SPECIAL: Celebrating the Strength of Women" celebrates the spirit of womanhood and the incredible strength of women in different walks of life.

"Valentine Special: Love in Different Forms" explores love in all its diverse forms, from romantic love to the love between friends and family.

In **"BACHAPAN: Nostalgic Memories of Childhood,"** I take you down memory lane to relive the beautiful moments of our childhood.

"FIRST DATE: A Memorable Beginning" is a heart-warming story of a couple's first date and the beautiful memories they create together.

"Mumbai Local: Tales of the City of Dreams" showcases the vibrant and diverse culture of Mumbai.

In **"NEW INDIA: A Journey of Hope and Transformation,"** I explore the changing landscape of India and the hope and transformation that comes with it.

"NIGHT SHIFT: An Unconventional Love Story" is a beautiful tale of love that blossoms in the most unexpected circumstances.

"Druvi: A Tale of Self-Discovery" is a story of a woman's journey of self-discovery and finding her true purpose in life.

In **"Love Story: A Journey of Two Hearts,"** I take you on a journey of two hearts and the trials and tribulations they face in their quest for love.

"THE MISSING: An Intriguing Mystery" is a gripping story of a missing person and the mystery surrounding their disappearance.

"Digital India: Bridging the Gap between the Past and Future," I explore the impact of technology on our lives and the changes it has brought to our society.

"Victory to Lord Rama," I share a personal reflection on the significance of Lord Rama and the lessons we can learn from his story. In "Advertisement," I explore the impact of marketing on our daily lives and the importance of being mindful of its effects.

"The Quest for Talent" is a story that delves into the struggles we face when pursuing our passions and the importance of perseverance. "Following a Daily Routine" offers a practical perspective on the benefits of establishing and maintaining a daily routine.

"Suicide," I touch on a sensitive topic and offer a reflection on the devastating effects of suicide, and the importance of seeking help and support during difficult times.

Finally, in **"To Provide Convenience to the Common Man"** is a story that highlights the importance of considering the needs of others when making decisions, while "Helping people around you" emphasizes the value of extending a helping hand to those around us.

I hope these stories will resonate with you and inspire you to reflect on your own life and experiences. Thank you for giving me the opportunity to share my thoughts with you.

Get ready to immerse yourself in these captivating stories that will take you on a rollercoaster ride of emotions and leave you wanting more.

Sincerely,

[Samanwit Kumar]

Oh life, oh life, where are you?

Oh life, oh life, where are you? I search for you in the depths of the ocean, and in the fast-flowing air, where are you?

Oh life, oh life, where are you? I search for you at the peak of mountains and in the flow of rivers, where are you?

I search for you in the pain and happiness of people, where are you?

I search for you in sky-high buildings, small houses, and huts, where are you?

I search for you in a little smile and in joy, where are you?

I search for you in heavy noise, full traffic jams, and empty streets, where are you?

I search for you in the world of music and in temples, where are you?

I search for you in my extensive library and my old memories, where are you?

I search for you in my old home and my new one, where are you? Oh life, oh life, where are you?

I search for you in the sparkly night and the dark starry night, where are you?

I also search for you deep in the forest and in long caves, where are you?

I search for you from the bottom of my heart and deep in my brain, where are you? Where are you? Oh life, oh life,

I also search for you in the caves of artists and in the characters of paintings, where are you?

Contents

MAA:
A Mother's Unconditional Love

Hey Sid, today I want to share with you not just a story, but a feeling that comes from the person who loves you more than anyone, your mother.

There are many characteristics in a woman's life, but according to me, being a mother is the best, and God is proud to have created this role.

One time, I was traveling from Mumbai to Calcutta for some official work during the rainy season.

I was staying at my friend's apartment, which was close to my office, and there was an older couple, who were like my parents, living there.

My mother had passed away from cancer the previous year. I remember that one night when I came back to the apartment, it was pouring rain outside.

My friends were on vacation, and suddenly I developed a high fever. I tried to call for help, but my body was too weak, and I couldn't move.

I didn't think I would make it through the night. Then I received a call on my mobile phone. I quickly picked up and asked for help, then fell asleep.

When I woke up the next day, I saw that the older lady, who I called MAA, was sitting beside me and had her hand on my head. She asked me if I was feeling better, and I replied yes, MAA.

She then left, telling my friend to take care of me. Later, my friend told me that the aunty had saved my life that night.

"**W**omen bear pain from the day they are born until the end. We celebrate festivals to remember their history, which is why we have been celebrating them for many years.

However, we tend to forget about the significance of the day once the celebrations are over, just like International Women's Day.

On this day, everyone talks about women from top to bottom, but eventually forgets about it with time.

I don't think there has been a significant change in the way our society thinks about women, but there has been an upgrade in the system from the old era to the new era of women.

Harassment is still present, but the way it happens has changed over time. Today, women speak up against it, whereas in the past, they endured attacks without uttering a word.

We acknowledge all the contributions made by women on special occasions, but we fail to follow through on what we say.

The question always arises, when will it stop? We all know the status of women in our country, and we cannot deny it. If we do not recognize it now, the consequences could be dire in the future."

VALENTINE SPECIAL:
Love in Different Forms

Love never dies. If you truly love someone, every day is like Valentine's Day for them. This is my story, which I will share with you.

My name is Kartik, and I belong to a middle-class family. I don't have any siblings, as my parents only wanted me.

They always wanted me to do something that would make them proud. So, they enrolled me in the best school in town, where I excelled in academics, sports, and love.

In high school, just before Valentine's Day, I first saw her - Gunjan.

Her beauty was out of this world, and many guys wanted to be friends with her.

I wanted more - I wanted to be with her. At that time, I had a girlfriend who gave me all the information about Gunjan, like her family details.

I tried many times to be friends with her but failed. She knew what I was up to, but still looked at me every day.

One day, I finally had the courage to ask her to be my friend, but all she did was smile and leave without a word.

I was disheartened, but after two days, she came to me and accepted my friendship. We started dating, and everything was going great between us. After a year, on Valentine's Day, I kissed her for the first time.

We grew together, made memories, and went to college together. On another Valentine's Day, she revealed to me that she was a cancer patient and was in her last stage.

She was the first person who wanted to give herself to me entirely.

She loved me, and she wanted me to be hers entirely. She also told me that she won't be there when I come back from studying abroad.

I was devastated and angry, but I couldn't change anything.

She asked me to build a hospital for cancer patients, so they could feel secure and given hope.

I held her close and celebrated our love together. Today, she is no longer with me, but her love and her wish live on.

The multinational hospital named after her provides love, support, care, and the best treatment for patients like her.

BACHAPAN:
Nostalgic Memories of Childhood

In the growing digital world, we have somehow lost children's childhood. Nowadays, if a child wants to know something, they learn it through a mobile device.

When a child cries, the parent gives them a phone or a tablet to keep them occupied.

Children either watch animated shows or listen to music, which makes them curious and fascinated.

The adrenaline rush, mischief, and excitement we had in our generation and before are lost.

The pressure-free life of just having fun and the fascination to learn anything and everything is lost.

One day, during my summer vacation at the age of 7 or 8, I visited my village, and my friend and I roamed around all day talking to people, helping them, and interacting with other kids.

While roaming, we found a field covered in dry grass and thought we could burn it for fun.

From that day on, we set it on fire, watched it burn, and then ran away before anyone could find us.

We were amused and excited. Our parents found out through someone that two boys had set a lot of dry grass on fire, and it was us.

The next time they saw us, they scolded us severely and even beat us. But what mattered to us was that we enjoyed it.

We were happy. We were mischievous. And that is childhood, not the childhood that today's children know.

We never had technology for fun.

Maybe they will be more advanced than us, but they will never know the actual joy of childhood.

FIRST DATE:
A Memorable Beginning

Riya Sen, I am from a simple family. My father is a government employee, my mother is a housewife, and I have a three-year-old cute brother.

I am currently studying in the best school, which is also my dream school. I was excited to join and attend my first day. I have always been a social person, and I think that has helped me blossom in school.

Through the years, I made a lot of friends and memories, but in between all of this, I met a certain special person.

We have known each other since my first day at school, and we often talk casually.

His name was Rahul, and he was an amazing man. I told my best friend, Shreya, everything about him. We never hide anything from each other; everything is crystal clear between us.

When I told her, she helped me get ready for my date.

5:30 p.m. Barista Café – that was the place where I was going to have my first date.

I was nervous, and my nerves were skyrocketing.

It felt like I was going for my first interview rather than my first date.

I took three hours to get ready, from which I took one and a half hours to calm my nerves. As I made my way to the Café, an auto-rickshaw splashed me with mud water, and my outfit was ruined from head to toe.

I was frustrated as I was getting late for my date, and my dress was ruined, but I went to meet him anyway.

On seeing me all drenched and tired, Rahul was shocked and asked me what happened. After listening to the entire story, he nodded and was silent. And that is how my first date became my worst date.

Mumbai Local:
Tales of the City of Dreams

Hey, I am the Mumbai Local - the breath of Mumbai, or you can say the heart of Mumbai. Every day, millions of people travel from the western suburbs and harbour using me.

From morning until night, I am in constant motion. I take some rest, but not like you guys.

There is no holiday for me. People travel with me from far and wide, chasing their dreams. They take a risk by traveling with me, especially during rush hour. Sometimes, I feel proud to be a part of it, but at other times, I feel bad.

This is because many people have died due to silly mistakes while traveling with me, putting their valuable lives at risk.

There are many advantages and disadvantages to me. I know that I am made by humans, but I don't understand nature. Time is valuable for me. If you miss me, then maybe you miss something that you really need.

People from all walks of life travel with me, and I don't judge human nature. It happens at any time, whether sad, happy, joyous, fun, etc. But people love me, always.

NEW INDIA:
A Journey of Hope and Transformation

We are looking for a new journey or a new world, but don't you think it's just the beginning of the end? The status of our country is very poor, but according to our politicians, it doesn't affect India. It's a big question for our next generation.

There are 4 million people unemployed, and this number increases day by day, but who cares about these things? Everybody in the country thinks only about themselves and not about the country.

Is this the new India that we are hoping for, or what we will give to our next generation? God told us that he made people, but what people have made can only destroy the world one day.

Today, competition is very high, and everyone wants to earn and learn to be at the top by hook or by crook. Today, death is uncertain, and it can come at any age for any reason, so there is no need to panic about it.

Sometimes we are proud to be Indian, but sometimes we feel ashamed when our people do dirty work.

We feel that we have a nice impact on the world, but there are some categories where some are proud, and some are laughing at us.

There is uncertainty spread throughout India that nobody is equal now.

Because those people who sit at the top don't want to sit beside or lift those who come from a lower class.

They don't want to help them come up, so this problem will never end, and it is going on year after year.

Chapter 1

Today, we live in a new India, also known as the 21st century. However, we must ask ourselves if this is truly a new era where we can see a brighter future for our next generation. If we compare our current state to that of 70 or 80 years ago, we can see that we are living in a healthier environment and atmosphere.

Our lives are relatively stress-free, and we do not have to worry about diseases like we did in the past.

Yet, it is said that change is the rule of nature, and we have certainly changed.

Although we have access to all the modern facilities and conveniences, we have lost touch with the joy of life.

We are constantly racing against time without knowing how much of it we have left.

Moreover, as we focus on capturing the Western world, we are slowly forgetting our own culture.

There are many things that we can compare between the old and new India. In the past, news was spread through newspapers, but now it is shared instantly through digital platforms like WhatsApp.

Similarly, political speeches used to hold little importance, but even a single word uttered today can make a big difference. To be continued in the next part... New India Chapter 2.

Chapter 2

What is the status of our country, or where do we stand and what do we stand for? Of course, today we are moving forward towards the next generation, but don't you think about what we will give to our next-generation: pollution, population, poverty, and a dirty atmosphere.

We spend a large amount of money on our development and system but do not think about where the money goes.

The rich become richer, the poor become poorer, and our leaders only keep giving us hope but do not fulfil it. For millions of years, our elders have told us that before men, there were monkeys who further evolved into men.

We are still monkeying; the only difference is that we are educated.

Nobody thinks about the people of the country; they just think about themselves, which has now become human nature.

There are 99% bad people in the world; if they ever get the power of command in their hands, they will destroy the world immediately. But only 1% of people keep the world alive. 10% of people in INDIA contribute to humanity in many ways,

but sometimes, they deliver it in the wrong place where it is not useful.

There are many categories in India like lower class, middle class, upper-middle class, high-class, and upper-high class. But it is not a mistake made by people; it's an illusion of Kaliyuga.

It is the second phase of Kaliyuga, and there is a total of six phases. In one phase, there are 1000 years, and we are at the second, with 4000 years remaining.

So, now you think about where we are, what we are, and where we should focus.

NIGHT SHIFT:
An Unconventional Love Story

Today, I am here on stage just because of God's grace, and it happened just a year ago. At that time, I was a regular worker like you, with lots of troubles in life.

When my wife and I came to the city in search of a job, we had to stay in a small room.

My name is Shankar, and I belong to a poor family. We always worked daily, but sometimes it did not fulfil our daily needs.

That's why I came to the city with big dreams, but when I faced reality, I realized it was not as easy as I thought it would be.

After a few days, I got a job as a security guard, even though I was not ready for it. But due to some circumstances, I accepted the job.

I told them not to put me on the night shift, and if there was an emergency, I would think about it.

Time passed, and we were gradually getting into a better situation. I paid off all my debts.

However, during those days, my wife got pregnant, and I admitted her to a good hospital because I didn't want to take any risks. After some time, she gave birth to a baby girl, and I felt proud and out of the world.

However, there was a burden on my shoulders after that medical incident, and I had to take on night shifts.

My duty was to keep an eye on a bungalow where I sat for eight hours, starting from 10:30 pm until morning at 7:30 am. I remember that night even today.

It was around 1:45 am when a speeding car came and hit an electrical pole.

When I went to see what had happened, I found the driver dead on the spot.

There was a bag in the back of the car, and it was open by chance.

When I opened the bag, I was shocked to see a huge amount of money. Nobody was around, and I took the bag with me.

After some time, I called the police, and they came and did their work. After investigating, they found that the driver was a criminal who had been on the run from the police for a long time.

He was dead. I told my wife about the incident, and we decided to use the money slowly and gradually. We have reached this stage because of that money.

That night shift changed my life forever.

DRUVI:
A Tale of Self-Discovery

A story about a girl whose father is a landlord. When Druvi was born, their family was so happy.

Mostly her father spread lots of sweets and clothes. He was a famous personality in his area, and people always respected him.

Her mother was a housewife, and she had two elder brothers who studied in the city.

When she was just ten years old, her father died because of a big loss in his business, and her mom was paralyzed by shock.

With time, the servant who used to work under him became the landlord.

Her father had started a business by taking a loan from the bank, but they lost in the business, which was a big change in her life. But she never lost hope and started working under the new landlord who acquired her property on a salary basis.

She requested the landlord not to disclose their secret with her brothers.

The landlord had one son who studied abroad. He understood the situation and agreed.

Druvi was also a hard worker with a sharp mind. She completed her studies while working and gathered lots of knowledge.

She had some targets in her life, which were to make her brother become good people and make her father's dream come true. The story of how Druvi accomplished her dreams will be in the next book.

Love Story:
A Journey of Two Hearts

(This All stories Belong to True Event only character have been changed to According to demand.)

This story is about an 18-year-old guy named Reshbha, who was a fresher in a medical college. He was filled with excitement for the new journey he had started alone and far from home.

With the confidence of his parents that he would fulfil all his dreams and make them proud, he aimed for success.

Everything was going on in the right way; in the first year, he secured the top position in college, and all the teachers and friends in coaching loved him.

After some time, he joined Facebook and made a girlfriend named Riya with whom he started chatting. Nobody knew about their relationship, and they continued to chat, date, and meet, which affected his studies and relationships with family and friends. They even had sex.

His parents did not know what was going on and wanted to talk to him, but he only said that he would give them a surprise soon.

One day, while chatting with Riya, he told her that he wanted to marry her as soon as possible. However, she refused and asked him to complete his studies and stand on his feet.

Reshbha was not ready to listen to any excuses, and he only wanted a yes from her. Riya was unaware of the negative affect her denial was having on Reshbha.

In shock, he committed suicide while being online with Riya. She tried to stop him, but he did not listen.

When his parents entered his room after breaking the door, they found him hanging from the fan with letters and gifts from Riya that said, "I Love You, Riya". Coming soon in the next book...

This story belongs to a middle-class couple who have been married for the past two years - Karan and Kajal. Karan works in a small company that provides him with a basic salary from which he tries to fulfil the dreams of his wife, Kajal.

Despite their arranged marriage, their relationship has turned into love over the past two years.

Karan is a simple man who doesn't believe in following trends, whether it's fashion or lifestyle, while Kajal desires a lavish life with a handsome husband.

However, with Karan's limited income, Kajal's dreams remain unfulfilled.

One day, they heard a commotion outside and saw a handsome man with incredible looks moving in front of their house.

Kajal became curious about him and took the opportunity to get to know him when Karan left for work.

They started spending time together whenever Karan was not around, and Kajal fell in love with him.

However, she didn't realize that the man she left her family for was a collector of girls for female traffickers.

He was just using her to make money. What will happen to her? Coming soon in the next book.

THE MISSING:
An Intriguing Mystery

Mita, a 20-year-old medical student, lived in Mumbai with her family. Her father, an ex-Army officer, was soon to be retired, and her mother was a social worker who was usually busy. Nita, her elder sister, lived abroad.

Mita, as an individual, grew up to be very smart and independent.

She had some casual affairs while she was studying in college, but nothing was serious as she didn't want to commit.

Her father often asked her to get married before continuing her studies, but she was against it as she wasn't ready for such a big step.

But what she didn't know was that everything was going to change.

Her family was on vacation when they met the Mathur. Their son, Aarav, was also a student who was pursuing his higher studies in the US.

She did not know anything about Aarav. To her, he was just the son of her father's friend.

Coming back from the break, Mita joined a firm where she worked to save up some money for her further studies, which she wanted to continue abroad. Nita offered her a job, but Mita refused as she wanted to do it on her own.

While she was working there, she met a guy, Pratik. Working in the same organization, they used to see each other quite a lot, and soon that simple conversation turned into something more.

Their friendship turned into feelings that further evolved into love. That love grew day by day, so much that Mita requested her father to allow her to marry the man she loves, Pratik.

After some convincing and a few meetings with Pratik, Mita's family finally granted permission and then fixed a date for the marriage.

Pratik and Mita's happiness knew no bounds. With all that was happening, they both felt ecstatic. The days passed by with heavy preparation, and a big fat Indian wedding of Pratik and Mita was here.

On the day of their honeymoon, they booked the best hotel, and the excitement Mita felt couldn't be controlled.

Shimla was a magical place, but what happened there left Mita with trauma. Pratik drank a lot on the first night of their honeymoon and slept before Mita.

When she woke up the next day, she couldn't find him. She waited for a few hours, thinking he'll return, but she saw no signs of Pratik. She asked the receptionist, people around, and even in the hotel's dining area, but no one saw him. She panicked and called her father.

When she narrated what had happened, he brushed it off, not believing her and saying that Pratik would be back. But she couldn't calm her nerves.

When no one believed her, she reported her husband's disappearance to the police.

The case investigator, Mr. Jadhav, asked for the entire story, and she narrated it the best she could. When the team of police officers started their investigation by calling all their friends, family, and acquaintances, Mita's father received a call.

He believed his daughter, and the severity of the case was building as the hours were passing.

He rushed to Shimla to console his daughter and tried to give her hope that Pratik would be found very soon.

Or will he? The answers will be found in the upcoming book.

DIGITAL INDIA:
Bridging the Gap between the Past and Future

The Benefits and Drawbacks of the Internet (Proper Use of the Internet for Success, Misuse of the Internet for Failure)

It is said that ever since man's arrival to God, he has been plagued with worries, whether he is born from his mother's womb or after coming to this earth. His worries never leave him, whether he is poor or rich.

Today, we will tell you a story about our 'Birju Maharaj', who started digital India. It is not easy; there was a time when we thought that nothing would come of it, but brother, the one who finds a new shore is the one who swims in the river.

So, let us start from the beginning and tell you the story of our digital India. It all started from a small village in Banaras, where the family was insistent on having a son, and the country needed it too. But my mother only wanted a son, and finally, my arrival happened.

My brother was so happy with my arrival that he distributed sweets at a wedding. Slowly but surely, our

Birju Maharaj started growing up, and he was now even known by name.

When it came to education, my father had to withdraw me from school, but the teacher left on his own accord. Time passed and Birju grew up, but he was not fortunate enough to receive an education.

However, luck was on his side in the form of a good friendship that gradually began to reveal to him that he did not belong where he was. He needed to get out of there, and that's exactly what happened when my older brother took him away.

As the bus started its journey to the big city, I remember thinking to myself where I could find a place to hide my head. A new journey had begun, and my brother knew where we were headed, but I had no idea as it was impossible to ask anyone as if it were an Olympic race.

We then decided to stop for a betel leaf, and perhaps this would be an opportunity to find out where we were going. As it turned out, the betel leaf seller was from our village, and we learned that he lived in a small place, which was as big as a room for us.

Nevertheless, it didn't matter because we were going to stay there, and people said that if we could arrange food and shelter in the city, everything else would gradually fall into place.

Now it was time to find work, and even though I had no formal education, it didn't matter because I found a job through a friend. I made new friends, and everyone had a mobile phone, which was a great thing.

At that time, buying something for Birju meant having to work harder, but as they say, every cloud has a silver lining. Our Birju Maharaj was caught in bad company, and I was left to deal with the consequences and the hassle of going to jail. My brother had left for work when the police arrived that night. They managed to catch everyone except our Birju, who was too smart for them.

But the police didn't give up, and they were determined to catch him. They finally caught him after eight long nights. The poor thing had been locked up for so long that society had forgotten about him.

But on the eighth night, someone finally came to bail him out. It was the neighbour from next door who had done a good deed, but unfortunately, they were not the best company. My brother was released, but his association with them was not so easily shaken off.

One day, they set out again after drinking, but this time they managed to escape without getting caught by the police. They were running at their own pace when our brother Birju fell in love with a commoner.

Now, what's done is done, but there was a little confusion. Payment was made, but the guy who paid was very smart and intelligent. Whatever he said, we had to follow. We just had to shake our heads and the matter would be resolved.

But we also wanted to understand a little bit. After all, what is this mobile phone that allows us to talk instantly even when we're far away? We also had to learn from him and give credit where credit is due.

Now, Birju told his friend "Nayansukh," whom he had given some work to do, that we also want to learn everything that he knows, so we can talk to him about everything, for the sake of "Nayansukh."

So, the two of them arrived and met a man named "Champak," who wasn't very knowledgeable about everything, but he was very fast and efficient in dealing with individual things. He kept a record of everything.

Her advice was that if we want to learn how to drive, we must use a car. Similarly, if we want to learn how to use a mobile phone, we need to buy one. So, what's the solution, brother? We must buy a mobile phone, but it's not that easy. Buying a phone means we'll have to put a sim card in it and the expenses will increase.

But it's okay, if we love something, we must bear the expense and adjust. He'll have to take some money from home because he won't get enough support. So, he should add some money and get a card.

Then, we started getting a lot of information from friends about the various features of different phones. It was time to get a phone number, and he did. But before the conversation was over, he had to recharge the balance.

At that time, a company started selling the cheapest phone, saying that a mobile phone should be in every hand. As soon as they started, the prices of all the phones went down and he bought a cheap phone where incoming calls were free, and he only had to pay for outgoing calls.

But the story was not over yet, because the expenses that the government was incurring were not being covered by the money they had. They thought of doing something big, but they didn't know what.

Once again, Mani was advised by his friends to collect some items from somewhere and contact the person in front of him on the phone. They reached their destination, but before the phone rang, the police arrived, and they were caught up in a series of serious crimes that resulted in them being sent to jail for a long time.

Now, who will help them in jail? But there is always someone whose owner is up there, and if you have done even a little good in your life, you will also receive its rewards. And that is exactly what happened. The one they were waiting for to join them arrived, and she would help them get out of jail. She asked Birju what he wanted to do and what needed to be done, because there is always a way to do any work, and the way they were doing it was wrong. Look, I know you love me very much, but this is not the way to move forward.

There is advice given in jail. Please think about what you need to do and how to do it. There must be a goal in life that we need to reach because life does not run on ice, and we must lose something to gain something.

Time is very powerful, so don't waste it. Please do something that won't make me ashamed of you, so that you can be proud of yourself.

Birju had decided that he needed to do something now that he had set his sights high. He went back to his friends and asked for help in starting a business, no matter how small it may be. With their help, he opened a small mobile phone shop. As the years went by, mobile phones became smartphones and Birju's business grew. One day, while at the market, Birju saw a man holding a big phone, and he asked him what it was.

The man replied that it was called the internet and that the future belonged to it. That night, Birju thought about what he had heard and the next morning, he decided to keep smartphones in his shop.

This decision brought in more customers and they started buying his products along with SIM cards.

But we had a lot of time, and the work done by the log was much more expensive than the internet, but those who thought so would recharge lightly, whether it benefited or not.

At that time, a new era came into the market, a revolution where free main data like everything new had never happened before.

Then with the help of the internet, he started a lot of businesses like online shopping, online education, online business, etc.

But after earning a lot of money, he thought that while money could do everything, he should do something for the people of the country like social security facilities (gas booking, police complaints, any kind of government assistance, etc.).

WORK 1>> So, he spoke to the government and launched a website (app) which listed the names of all top-ranking officials in various departments of the government such as police, hospitals, politicians, etc.

He also built an escalation matrix, so if you live in the Versova area of Andheri in Mumbai and need police help, you can directly contact the area's inspector and the response time will be tracked. If a response is not received within 5 minutes, then the boss will be automatically contacted.

If the boss does not respond, then the escalation will go to the boss's boss and the chain will continue up to the PRIME MINISTER. But there is no need to go that high because everything can be easily resolved since everyone loves their job.

Then the world changed, and every task was completed easily and on time with new speed.

WORK 2>> Birju Maharaj brought about many changes, including creating a new identity card.

He went to the passport office to create a PAN card, but then a few days later, he had to get an Aadhaar card, then a passport, a driving license, and so on. Carrying and making so many documents was very difficult.

Then, the government came to his rescue and consolidated everything into a single smart card.

Now, every person is provided with a unique number containing all their information.

They no longer must carry separate documents. Birju Maharaj became the face of Digital India and saw how we can access anything through the internet, regardless of location. With the help of the internet, we can access anything from anywhere in the world. After this, Birju got married and had children. His small shop became Birju Mohan and Sons, with ten branches in pure urban areas. He himself spoke about Digital India's nakedness.

"Victory to Lord Rama"

L ord Rama remains the same in both joy and sorrow. All people should strive to maintain an equilibrium in both happiness and sorrow because these states are impermanent.

If there is sorrow, there will also be an awareness of happiness, and in the same way, when happiness comes, there will also be an awareness of sorrow.

Those who can maintain themselves equally in these two situations are the ones who know how to live life in its fullest and achieve greatness.

"Advertisement"

Nowadays, advertisements are not realistic.

Take the example of washing powder advertisements, which show that all stains will be completely removed. But these types of stains are not seen by anyone anymore, or if they are, it is only seen by workers or laborers who cannot afford such expensive powders.

In other words, the powder may remove stubborn stains, but stubborn stains are usually found on the clothes of the working-class people who cannot afford expensive powders.

They cannot buy these powders, and the ones who can afford them are the ones whose clothes are not that dirty.

"The Quest for Talent"

In our country, there are many talents that reside in villages or small places.

It is easy to find such talent if you search for it, just like if you were looking for a swimmer in a village, you could easily find a young and untrained swimmer.

Similarly, search for talent and provide them with good training to help them progress.

This way, we can find truly talented people and help them reach their potential.

"Following a Daily Routine"

Have you ever heard of a farmer or labourer getting diabetes, high blood pressure? I don't think so. But people who work in offices or have a better lifestyle are the ones who suffer from these diseases because we do not pay attention to our food, drink, and physical exercise.

Another thing is that the fort of Shivaji Maharaj was built many years ago.

It is still as strong as it was then, but nowadays, talented/specialist people who build buildings must do redevelopment after 10-15 years.

"To Provide Convenience to the Common Man

Nowadays, there are many schemes introduced to provide convenience to the common man.

However, the common man is not aware of all these schemes, and therefore, before introducing any scheme, it is necessary to provide maximum knowledge to them about it.

After providing knowledge, if the common man avails of that scheme, please provide him with the necessary assistance and convenience until the end.

Just like nowadays, sales and marketing teams keep following up until the product is sold, but once it is sold, they don't bother to look back.

My point is that nowadays, we should focus more on service than sales because if you become number one in providing service, soon your sales numbers will also become number one.

"Suicide"

The pain of suicide is felt most by those who commit it, as their soul always wanders in darkness.

Even when we face a conflict, separation, or abandonment, the pain we experience is nothing compared to what those who commit suicide feel.

They remain lost in darkness, able to see everyone, but no one can see or hear their pain. They suffer, not knowing with whom they can share their grief, which leads them to take their own life.

Imagine yourself wandering in the darkness, unable to share your thoughts with anyone. What could be more painful than that?

Therefore, before committing suicide, think about whether you want to experience more pain than you already have.

"Helping people around you"

From childhood to this day, if you look back at your journey, you are not alone, you have met many people such as school friends, teachers, shopkeepers, and anyone else you recognize and who also knows you.

So, if you ever achieve something in life, don't forget to help those people who have fallen behind in the race of life.

By doing this, you will feel a different kind of joy.

Dear valued customer,

We are thrilled to announce that 100% of the profits from the sale of our book of multiple stories will be donated to a charity trust. The author will not receive any portion of the profits.

Our goal is to not only provide an enjoyable reading experience for our customers but also to make a positive impact in the world. We believe that supporting charitable causes is an important way to do this.

By purchasing our book, you will not only be supporting the author's work but also contributing to a worthy cause. Your purchase will help to make a difference in the lives of those in need.

We believe that giving back to the community is a responsibility that we all share. We hope that our commitment to donating all profits from the sale of our book will inspire others to do the same.

Thank you for your support.

Sincerely,

[Samanwit Kumar]

Dear valued customer,

We are thrilled to offer you a fast and secure payment option for purchasing our book of multiple stories using blockchain technology, specifically Shib Inu and Bitcoin cryptocurrencies.

Using blockchain technology enables us to offer you a decentralized and secure payment option, where your transaction is recorded on a public ledger that is not controlled by any single entity, providing you with a level of security and transparency that traditional payment methods cannot match.

By choosing to use Shib Inu or Bitcoin cryptocurrency for your purchase, you can enjoy fast and efficient processing of your payment, with lower transaction fees compared to other payment methods. Additionally, using blockchain technology ensures that your payment is not subject to the same risks associated with centralized payment processing, such as fraud or hacking.

We are committed to providing you with a convenient and secure payment experience, and we believe that using blockchain technology with Shib Inu and Bitcoin cryptocurrencies is the way to achieve this. We appreciate your business, and we hope that this new payment option will enhance your experience purchasing our book.

Thank you for your support.

Sincerely,

[Samanwit Kumar]

Dear valued customer,

Shib Inu is a cryptocurrency that is built on the Ethereum blockchain. It is a decentralized and secure payment method that uses blockchain technology to provide a fast and efficient transaction processing system.

Using Shib Inu as a payment method for purchasing our book of multiple stories offers several advantages. Firstly, it provides a decentralized and secure payment system, where your transaction is recorded on a public ledger that is not controlled by any single entity, providing you with a level of security and transparency that traditional payment methods cannot match.

Secondly, using Shib Inu for your purchase offers fast and efficient processing of your payment, with lower transaction fees compared to other payment methods. This is because blockchain technology allows for direct peer-to-peer transactions without the need for intermediaries.

Finally, using Shib Inu as a payment method ensures that your payment is not subject to the same risks associated with centralized payment processing, such as fraud or hacking.

Overall, using Shib Inu as a payment method offers a convenient and secure way to purchase our book of multiple stories. We believe that using blockchain technology and Shib Inu cryptocurrency is the way to achieve a fast, efficient, and secure payment experience for our valued customers.

Thank you for your support.

Sincerely,

[Samanwit Kumar]

<THE END>